Donald Trump
Biography & Quotes

Introduction

Donald John Trump (born June 14, 1946) is the 45th and current president of the United States. Before entering politics, he was a businessman and television personality.

Born and raised in Queens, New York City, Trump attended Fordham University for two years and received a bachelor's degree in economics from the Wharton School of the University of Pennsylvania. He became president of his father Fred Trump's real estate business in 1971, renamed it The Trump Organization, and expanded its operations to building or renovating skyscrapers, hotels, casinos, and golf courses. Trump later started various side ventures, mostly by licensing his name. Trump and his businesses have been involved in more than 4,000 state and federal legal actions, including six bankruptcies. He owned the Miss Universe brand of beauty pageants from 1996 to 2015, and produced and hosted the reality television series The Apprentice from 2004 to 2015.

Trump's political positions have been described as populist, protectionist, isolationist, and nationalist.

He entered the 2016 presidential race as a Republican and was elected in a surprise electoral college victory over Democratic nominee Hillary Clinton while losing the popular vote. He became the oldest first-term U.S. president and the first without prior military or government service. His election and policies have sparked numerous protests. Trump has made many false or misleading statements during his campaign and presidency. The statements have been documented by fact-checkers, and the media have widely described the phenomenon as unprecedented in American politics. Many of his comments and actions have been characterized as racially charged or racist.

During his presidency, Trump ordered a travel ban on citizens from several Muslim-majority countries, citing security concerns; after legal challenges, the Supreme Court upheld the policy's third revision. He enacted a tax-cut package for individuals and businesses, rescinding the individual health insurance mandate penalty of the Affordable Care Act (ACA), but has failed to repeal and replace the ACA as a whole. He appointed Neil Gorsuch, Brett Kavanagh and Amy Coney Barrett to the Supreme Court. In foreign policy, Trump has pursued an America First agenda, renegotiating the North American Free Trade Agreement (NAFTA) as the United States–Mexico–

Canada Agreement (USMCA) and withdrawing the U.S. from the Trans-Pacific Partnership trade negotiations, the Paris Agreement on climate change, and the Iran nuclear deal. He imposed import tariffs which triggered a trade war with China, moved the U.S. embassy in Israel to Jerusalem and withdrew U.S. troops from northern Syria. He met three times with North Korean leader Kim Jong-un, but talks on denuclearization broke down in 2019. He reacted slowly to the COVID-19 pandemic, downplayed the threat, ignored or contradicted many recommendations from health officials, and promoted false information about unproven treatments and the availability of testing.

A special counsel investigation led by Robert Mueller found that Trump and his campaign benefited from Russian interference in the 2016 presidential election, but did not find sufficient evidence to press charges of criminal conspiracy or coordination with Russia. Mueller also investigated Trump for obstruction of justice, and his report neither indicted nor exonerated Trump on that offense. After Trump solicited Ukraine to investigate his political rival Joe Biden, the House of Representatives impeached him in December 2019 for abuse of power and obstruction of Congress. The Senate acquitted him of both charges in February 2020.

Trump lost the 2020 presidential election to Biden but refused to concede defeat. He has made unsubstantiated accusations of electoral fraud, mounted a series of unsuccessful legal challenges to the results, and ordered government officials not to cooperate in the presidential transition.

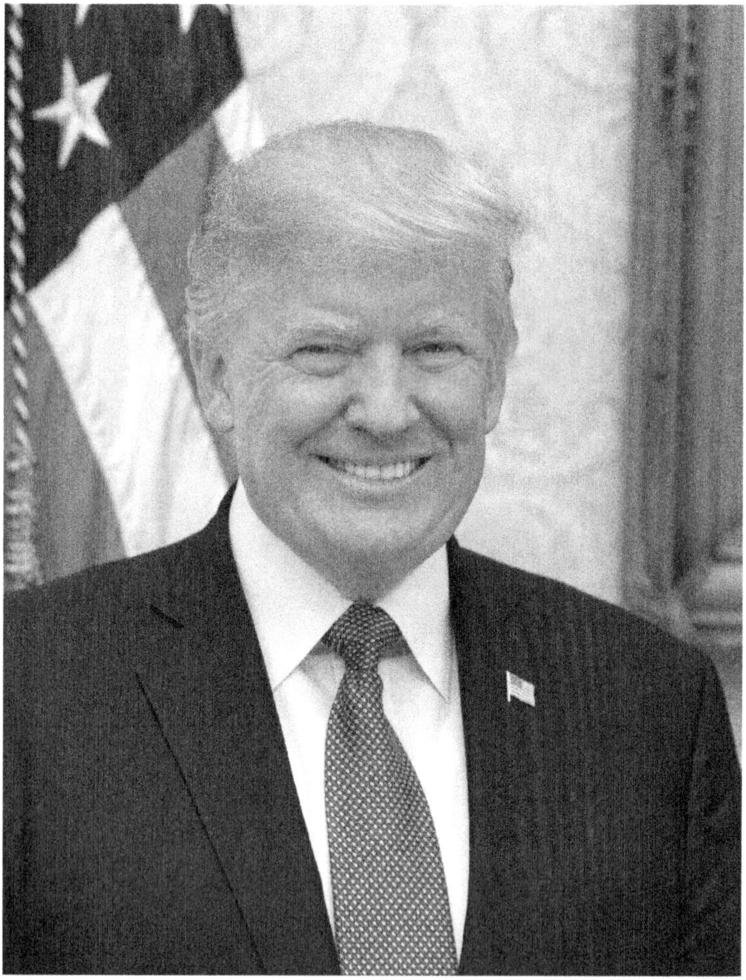

Personal life

Early life

Trump was born on June 14, 1946, at Jamaica Hospital in the borough of Queens, New York City. His father was Frederick Christ Trump, a Bronx-born real estate developer whose parents were German immigrants. His mother was Scottish-born housewife Mary Anne Macleod Trump. Trump grew up in the Jamaica Estates neighborhood of Queens and attended the Kew-Forest School from kindergarten through seventh grade. At age 13, he was enrolled in the New York Military Academy, a private boarding school. In 1964, he enrolled at Fordham University. Two years later he transferred to the Wharton School of the University of Pennsylvania, graduating in May 1968 with a B.S. in economics. Profiles of Trump published in The New York Times in 1973 and 1976 erroneously reported that he had graduated first in his class at Wharton, but he had never made the school's honor roll. In 2015, Trump's lawyer Michael Cohen threatened Fordham University and the New York Military Academy with legal action if they released Trump's academic records.

Military deferment

While in college, Trump obtained four student draft deferments. In 1966, he was deemed fit for military service based upon a medical examination, and in July 1968 a local draft board classified him as eligible to serve. In October 1968, he was medically deferred and classified 1-Y (unqualified for duty except in the case of a national emergency). In 1972, he was reclassified 4-F due to bone spurs, which permanently disqualified him from service.

Family

Parents and siblings

Fred Trump started working in real estate with his mother Elizabeth when he was 15, after his father Friedrich had died in the 1918 flu pandemic. By 1926, their company, "E. Trump & Son", was active in the New York boroughs of Queens and Brooklyn. It would grow to build and sell tens of thousands of houses, barracks, and apartments. Fred claimed to be Swedish amid the anti-German sentiment sparked by World War II; Trump also claimed Swedish heritage until 1990. Trump's mother Mary Anne MacLeod was born in Scotland. Fred and Mary were married in 1936 and raised their family in Queens. Trump grew up with three elder siblings – Maryanne, Fred Jr., and Elizabeth – and younger brother Robert.

Wives and children

In 1977, Trump married Czech model Ivana Zelnickova. They have three children, Donald Jr. (born 1977), Ivanka (born 1981), and Eric (born 1984), and ten grandchildren. Ivana became a naturalized United States citizen in 1988. The couple divorced in 1992, following Trump's affair with actress Marla

Maples. Maples and Trump married in 1993 and had one daughter, Tiffany (born 1993). They were divorced in 1999, and Tiffany was raised by Marla in California. In 2005, Trump married Slovenian model Melania Knauss. They have one son, Barron (born 2006). Melania gained U.S. citizenship in 2006.

Religion

Trump went to Sunday school and was confirmed in 1959 at the First Presbyterian Church in Jamaica, Queens. In the 1970s, his parents joined the Marble Collegiate Church in Manhattan, which belongs to the Reformed Church. The pastor at Marble, Norman Vincent Peale, ministered to Trump's family until Peale's death in 1993. Trump has described Peale as a mentor. In 2015, after Trump said he attends Marble, the church stated he "is not an active member" of the church. In November 2019, Trump appointed his personal pastor, televangelist Paula White, to the White House Office of Public Liaison. In October 2020, Trump said that he identified as a non-denominational Christian.

Health

Trump has called golfing his "primary form of exercise" but usually does not walk the course. He considers exercise a waste of energy, because he believes the body is "like a battery, with a finite amount of energy" which is depleted by exercise. In 2015, Harold Bornstein, who had been Trump's personal physician since 1980, wrote that Trump would "be the healthiest individual ever elected to the presidency" in a letter released by the Trump campaign. In 2018, Bornstein said Trump had dictated the contents of the letter and that three agents of Trump had removed his medical records in February 2017 without authorization.

Statements by White House physicians Ronny Jackson and Sean Conley in 2018, 2019, and 2020 said Trump was healthy overall, but was obese. Several outside cardiologists commented that Trump's 2018 LDL cholesterol level of 143 did not indicate excellent health. Trump's 2019 coronary CT calcium scan score indicates he suffers from a common form of coronary artery disease.

Trump was hospitalized with COVID-19 on October 2, 2020, and treated with the antiviral drug remdesivir, the steroid dexamethasone, and an unapproved experimental antibody drug made by Regeneron. He was discharged on October 5.

Wealth

In 1982, Trump was listed on the initial Forbes list of wealthy individuals as having a share of his family's estimated $200 million net worth. His financial losses in the 1980s caused him to be dropped from the list between 1990 and 1995. In its 2020 billionaires ranking, Forbes estimated Trump's net worth at $2.1 billion (1,001st in the world, 275th in the U.S.), making him one of the richest politicians in American history and the first billionaire American president. Forbes estimated that his net worth declined 31% and his ranking fell 138 spots between 2015 and 2018. When he filed mandatory financial disclosure forms with the Federal Elections Commission in July 2015, Trump claimed a net worth of about $10 billion however, FEC figures cannot corroborate this estimate because they only show each of his largest buildings as being worth over $50 million, yielding total assets worth more than $1.4 billion and debt over $265 million.

Journalist Jonathan Greenberg reported in 2018 that Trump, using the pseudonym "John Barron" and claiming to be a Trump Organization official, called him in 1984 to falsely assert that he owned "in excess of ninety percent" of the Trump family's business, to secure a higher ranking on the Forbes 400 list of wealthy Americans. Greenberg also wrote that Forbes had vastly overestimated Trump's wealth and wrongly included him on the Forbes 400 rankings of 1982, 1983, and 1984.

Trump has often said he began his career with "a small loan of one million dollars" from his father, and that he had to pay it back with interest. In October 2018, The New York Times reported that Trump "was a millionaire by age 8", borrowed at least $60 million from his father, largely failed to reimburse him, and had received $413 million (adjusted for inflation) from his father's business empire over his lifetime. According to the report, Trump and his family committed tax fraud, which a lawyer for Trump denied. The tax department of New York said it is investigating. Trump's investments underperformed the stock market and the New York property market. Forbes estimated in October 2018 that the value of Trump's personal brand licensing business had declined by 88% since 2015, to $3 million.

Trump's tax returns from 1985 to 1994 show net losses totaling $1.17 billion over the ten-year period, in contrast to his claims about his financial health and business abilities. The New York Times reported that "year after year, Mr. Trump appears to have lost more money than nearly any other individual American taxpayer," and Trump's "core business losses in 1990 and 1991 more than $250 million each year were more than double those of the nearest taxpayers in the I.R.S. information for those years". In 1995 his reported losses were $915.7 million.

According to a September 2020 analysis by The New York Times of twenty years of data from Trump's tax returns, Trump had accumulated hundreds of millions of U.S. dollars in losses, and deferred declaring $287 million in forgiven debt as taxable income. According to the analysis, Trump's main sources of income were his share of revenue from The Apprentice and income from businesses in which he was a minority partner, while his majority-owned businesses were largely running at losses. A significant portion of Trump's income was in tax credits due to his losses, which enables him to avoid paying income tax, or paying as little as $750, for several years. Over the past decade, Trump has been balancing his businesses' losses by selling and taking out loans against assets, including a $100 million mortgage on Trump Tower (due in 2022) and the liquidation of over $200 million in stocks and bonds. Trump has personally guaranteed $421 million in debt, most of which is due to be repaid by 2024. If he is re-elected and unable to repay or refinance the debt, the lenders may consider foreclosing on a sitting president, an unprecedented situation. The tax records also showed Trump had unsuccessfully pursued business deals in China, including by developing a partnership with a major government-controlled company.

Trump has a total of over $1 billion in debts, borrowed to finance his assets, reported Forbes in October 2020. Around $640 million or more was owed to various banks and trust organizations. Around $450 million was owed to unknown creditors. However, Trump's assets still out value his debts, reported Forbes.

Business career

Real estate

While a student at Wharton and after graduating in 1968, Trump worked at his father Fred's real estate company, Trump Management, which owned middle-class rental housing in New York City's outer boroughs. In 1971, he became president of the company and began using The Trump Organization as an umbrella brand. The business had previously used the names Fred C. Trump Organization, Fred Trump Organization, and Trump Organization, but had not had a single formal name. It was registered as a corporation in 1981.

Manhattan developments

Trump attracted public attention in 1978 with the launch of his family's first Manhattan venture, the renovation of the derelict Commodore Hotel, adjacent to Grand Central Terminal. The financing was facilitated by a $400 million city property tax abatement arranged by Fred Trump, who also joined Hyatt in guaranteeing $70 million in bank construction financing. The hotel reopened in 1980 as the Grand Hyatt Hotel, and that same year, Trump obtained rights to develop Trump Tower, a mixed-use skyscraper in Midtown Manhattan. The building houses the headquarters of the Trump Organization and was Trump's primary residence until 2019.

In 1988, Trump acquired the Plaza Hotel in Manhattan with a loan of $425 million from a consortium of banks. Two years later, the hotel filed for bankruptcy protection, and a reorganization plan was approved in 1992. In 1995, Trump lost the hotel to Citibank and investors from Singapore and Saudi Arabia, who assumed $300 million of the debt.

In 1996, Trump acquired a vacant 71-story skyscraper at 40 Wall Street. After an extensive renovation, the high-rise was renamed the Trump Building.[96] In the early 1990s, Trump won the right to develop a 70-acre (28 ha) tract in the Lincoln Square neighborhood near the Hudson River. Struggling with debt from other ventures in 1994, Trump sold most of his interest in the project to Asian investors who were able to finance completion of the project, Riverside South.

Palm Beach estate

In 1985, Trump acquired the Mar-a-Lago estate in Palm Beach, Florida. Trump used a wing of the estate as a home, while converting the remainder into a private club with an initiation fee and annual dues. In 2019, Trump declared Mar-a-Lago his primary residence.

Atlantic City casinos

In 1984, Trump opened Harrah's at Trump Plaza hotel and casino in Atlantic City, New Jersey, with financing from the Holiday Corporation, who also managed the operation. Gambling had been legalized there in 1977 to revitalize the once-popular seaside destination. The property's poor financial results worsened tensions between Holiday and Trump, who paid Holiday $70 million in May 1986 to take sole control of the property. Earlier, Trump had also acquired a partially completed building in Atlantic City from the Hilton Corporation for $320 million. Upon its completion in 1985, that hotel and casino were called Trump Castle. Trump's then-wife Ivana managed it until 1988.

Trump acquired a third casino in Atlantic City, the Trump Taj Mahal, in 1988 in a highly leveraged transaction. It was financed with $675 million in junk bonds and completed at a cost of $1.1 billion, opening in April 1990. The project went bankrupt the following year, and the reorganization left Trump with only half his initial ownership stake and required him to pledge personal guarantees of future performance. Facing "enormous debt", he gave up control of his money-losing airline, Trump Shuttle, and sold his megayacht, the Trump Princess, which had been indefinitely docked in Atlantic City while leased to his casinos for use by wealthy gamblers.

In 1995, Trump founded Trump Hotels & Casino Resorts (THCR), which assumed ownership of Trump Plaza, Trump Castle, and the Trump Casino in Gary, Indiana. THCR purchased the Taj Mahal in 1996 and underwent successive bankruptcies in 2004, 2009, and 2014, leaving Trump with only ten percent ownership. He remained chairman of THCR until 2009.

Golf courses

The Trump Organization began acquiring and constructing golf courses in 1999. It owned 16 golf courses and resorts worldwide and operated another two as of December 2016.

From his inauguration until the end of 2019, Trump spent around one of every five days at one of his golf clubs.

Branding and licensing

The Trump name has been licensed for various consumer products and services, including foodstuffs, apparel, adult learning courses, and home furnishings. According to an analysis by The Washington Post, there are more than fifty licensing or management deals involving Trump's name, which have generated at least $59 million in yearly revenue for his companies. By 2018, only two consumer goods companies continued to license his name.

Side ventures

In September 1983, Trump purchased the New Jersey Generals, a team in the United States Football League. After the 1985 season, the league folded, largely due to Trump's strategy of moving games to a fall schedule (where they competed with the NFL for audience) and trying to force a merger with the NFL by bringing an antitrust suit against the organization.

Trump's businesses have hosted several boxing matches at the Atlantic City Convention Hall adjacent to and promoted as taking place at the Trump Plaza in Atlantic City. In 1989 and 1990, Trump lent his name to the Tour de Trump cycling stage race, which was an attempt to create an American equivalent of European races such as the Tour de France or the Giro distalia.

In the late 1980s, Trump mimicked the actions of Wall Street's so-called corporate raiders, whose tactics had attracted wide public attention. Trump began to purchase significant blocks of shares in various public companies, leading some observers to think he was engaged in the practice called greenmail, or feigning the intent to acquire the companies and then pressuring management to repurchase the buyer's stake at a premium. The New York Times found that Trump initially made millions of dollars in such stock transactions, but later "lost most, if not all, of those gains after investors stopped taking his takeover talk seriously".

In 1988, Trump purchased the defunct Eastern Air Lines shuttle, with 21 planes and landing rights in New York City, Boston, and Washington, D.C. He financed the purchase with $380 million from 22 banks, rebranded the operation the Trump Shuttle, and operated it until 1992. Trump failed to earn a profit with the airline and sold it to USAir.

In 1992, Trump, his siblings Maryanne, Elizabeth, and Robert, and Cousin John W. Walter, each with a 20 percent share, formed All County Building Supply & Maintenance Corp. The company had no offices and is alleged to have been a shell company for paying the vendors providing services and supplies for Trump's rental units, and then billing those services and supplies to Trump Management with markups of 20–50 percent and more. The proceeds generated by the markups were shared by the owners. The increased costs were used as justification to get state approval for increasing the rents of Trump's rent-stabilized units.

From 1996 to 2015, Trump owned all or part of the Miss Universe pageants, including Miss USA and Miss Teen USA. Due to disagreements with CBS about scheduling, he took both pageants to NBC in 2002. In 2007, Trump received a star on the Hollywood Walk of Fame for his work as producer of Miss Universe. After NBC and Univision dropped the pageants from their broadcasting lineups in June 2015, Trump bought NBC's share of the Miss Universe Organization and sold the entire company to the William Morris talent agency.

Trump University

In 2004, Trump co-founded Trump University, a company that sold real estate training courses priced from $1,500 to $35,000. After New York State authorities notified the company that its use of the word "university" violated state law, its name was changed to Trump Entrepreneur Initiative in 2010.

In 2013, the State of New York filed a $40 million civil suit against Trump University; the suit alleged that the company made false statements and defrauded consumers. In addition, two class actions were filed in federal court against Trump and his companies. Internal documents revealed that employees were instructed to use a hard-sell approach, and former employees testified that Trump University had defrauded or lied to its students. Shortly after he won the presidency, Trump agreed to pay a total of $25 million to settle the three cases.

Foundation

The Donald J. Trump Foundation was a private foundation established in 1988. In the foundation's final years its funds mostly came from donors other than Trump, who did not donate any personal funds to the charity from 2009 until 2014. The foundation gave to health care and sports-related charities, as well as conservative groups.

In 2016, The Washington Post reported that the charity had committed several potential legal and ethical violations, including alleged self-dealing and possible tax evasion. Also in 2016, the New York State attorney General's office said the foundation appeared to be in violation of New York laws regarding charities and ordered it to immediately cease its fundraising activities in New York. Trump's team announced in December 2016 that the foundation would be dissolved.

In June 2018 the New York attorney general's office filed a civil suit against the foundation, Trump, and his adult children, seeking $2.8 million in restitution and additional penalties. In December 2018, the foundation ceased operation and disbursed all its assets to other charities. In November 2019, a New York state judge ordered Trump to pay $2 million to a group of charities for misusing the foundation's funds, in part to finance his presidential campaign.

Conflicts of interest

Before being inaugurated as president, Trump moved his businesses into a revocable trust run by his eldest sons and a business associate. According to ethics experts, this measure does not help avoid conflicts of interest, because Trump continues to profit from his businesses. Because Trump would have knowledge of how his administration's policies affect his businesses, ethics experts recommend selling the businesses. Though Trump said he would eschew "new foreign deals", the Trump Organization has since pursued expansions of its operations in Dubai, Scotland, and the Dominican Republic.

Pending lawsuits allege that Trump is violating the Domestic and Foreign Emoluments Clauses of the U.S. Constitution. The plaintiffs say that Trump's business interests could allow foreign governments to influence him. NBC News reported in 2019 that representatives of at least 22 foreign governments, including some facing charges of corruption or human rights abuses, appeared to have spent money at Trump Organization businesses during his presidency. The litigation marks the first time that the Emoluments Clauses have been substantively litigated in court. As president, Trump mocked the Emoluments Clause as "phony".

Media career

Books

Trump has written up to 19 books on business, financial, or political topics, though he has employed ghostwriters to actually write them. Trump's first book, The Art of the Deal (1987), was a New York Times Best Seller. While Trump was credited as co-author, the entire book was ghostwritten by Tony

Schwartz. According to The New Yorker, "The book expanded Trump's renown far beyond New York City, promoting an image of himself as a successful dealmaker and tycoon." Trump has called the book his second favorite after the Bible.

WWF/WWE

Trump has had a sporadic relationship with the professional wrestling promotion WWE (World Wrestling Entertainment) since the late 1980s. He was inducted into the celebrity wing of the WWE Hall of Fame in 2013. Most notably, he shaved Vince McMahon's head bald after Bobby Lashley represented him in a Hair vs. Hair match against Umaga at WWE's annual flagship event WrestleMania 23 in 2007.

The Apprentice

In 2003, Trump became the co-producer and host of The Apprentice, a reality show in which Trump played the role of a powerful chief executive and contestants competed for a year of employment at the Trump Organization. Trump winnowed out contestants with his famous catchphrase "You're fired". He later co-hosted The Celebrity Apprentice, in which celebrities competed to win money for charities.

Acting

Trump has made cameo appearances in eight films and television shows.

Talk shows

Starting in the 1990s, Trump was a guest about 24 times on the nationally syndicated Howard Stern Show. He also had his own short-form talk radio program called Trumped! (One to two minutes on weekdays) from 2004 to 2008. From 2011 until 2015, he was a weekly unpaid guest commentator on Fox & Friends.

Political career

Political activities up to 2015

Trump's political party affiliation changed numerous times. He registered as a Republican in Manhattan in 1987, switched to the Reform Party in 1999, the Democratic Party in 2001, and back to the Republican Party in 2009.

In 1987, Trump placed full-page advertisements in three major newspapers, advocating peace in Central America, accelerated nuclear disarmament talks with the Soviet Union, and reduction of the federal budget deficit by making American allies pay "their fair share" for military defense. He ruled out running for local office but not for the presidency.

2000 presidential campaign

In 1999, Trump filed an exploratory committee to seek the nomination of the Reform Party for the 2000 presidential election. A July 1999 poll matching him against likely Republican nominee George W. Bush and likely Democratic nominee Al Gore showed Trump with seven percent support. Trump dropped out of the race in February 2000.

2012 presidential speculation

Trump speculated about running against President Barack Obama in the 2012 election, making his first speaking appearance at the Conservative Political Action Conference (CPAC) in February 2011 and giving speeches in early primary states. In May 2011 he announced he would not run.

Trump's presidential ambitions were generally not taken seriously at the time. Before the 2016 election, The New York Times speculated that Trump "accelerated his ferocious efforts to gain stature within the political world" after Obama lampooned him at the White House Correspondents' Association Dinner in April 2011.

In 2011, the superintendent of the New York Military Academy at the time, Jeffrey Coverdale, ordered the headmaster of the school, Evan Jones, to give him Trump's academic records so he could keep them secret, according to Jones. Coverdale confirmed that he had been asked to hand the records over to members of the school's board of trustees who were Trump's friends, but he refused to and instead sealed them on campus. The incident reportedly happened days after Trump demanded the release of Obama's academic records.

2013–2015

In 2013, Trump spoke at CPAC again. He railed against illegal immigration, bemoaned Obama's "unprecedented media protection", advised against harming Medicare, Medicaid, and Social Security, and suggested the government "take" Iraq's oil and use the proceeds to pay a million dollars each to families of dead soldiers. He spent over $1 million that year to research a possible 2016 candidacy.

In October 2013, New York Republicans circulated a memo suggesting that Trump run for governor in 2014 against Andrew Cuomo. Trump responded that while New York had problems and its taxes were too high, he was not interested in the governorship. A poll showed Trump losing to the more popular Cuomo by 37 points in a hypothetical election.

Trump's attorney Michael Cohen said that he sent letters to the New York Military Academy and Fordham in May 2015, threatening legal action if the schools ever released Trump's grades or SAT scores. Fordham confirmed receipt of the letter as well as a phone call from a member of the Trump team.

2016 presidential campaign

On June 16, 2015, Trump announced his candidacy for President of the United States. His campaign was initially not taken seriously by political analysts, but he quickly rose to the top of opinion polls.

On Super Tuesday, Trump received the most votes, and he remained the front-runner throughout the primaries. After a landslide win in Indiana on May 3, 2016 – which prompted the remaining candidates Cruz and John Kasich to suspend their presidential campaigns – RNC chairman Reince Priebus declared Trump the presumptive Republican nominee.

General election campaign

Hillary Clinton had a significant lead over Trump in national polls throughout most of 2016. In early July, her lead narrowed in national polling averages.

Donald Trump and his running mate for vice president, Mike Pence. They appear to be standing in front of a huge screen with the colors of the American flag displayed on it. Trump is at the left, facing toward the viewer and making "thumbs-up" gestures. Pence is at right, facing Trump and clapping.

On July 15, 2016, Trump announced his selection of Indiana governor Mike Pence as his vice presidential running mate. Four days later, the two were officially nominated by the Republican Party at the Republican National Convention.

Trump and Clinton faced off in three presidential debates in September and October 2016. Trump's refusal to say whether he would accept the result of the election, regardless of the outcome, drew particular attention, with some saying it undermined democracy.

Campaign rhetoric

In his campaign, Trump said he disdained political correctness and frequently made claims of media bias. His fame and provocative statements earned him an unprecedented amount of free media coverage, elevating his standing in the Republican primaries.

Trump made a record number of false statements compared to other candidates; the press reported on his campaign lies and falsehoods, with the Los Angeles Times saying, "Never in modern presidential politics has a major candidate made false statements as routinely as Trump has." His campaign statements were often opaque or suggestive.

Trump adopted the phrase "truthful hyperbole", coined by his ghostwriter Tony Schwartz, to describe his public speaking style.

Support from the far right

According to Michael Barkun, the Trump campaign was remarkable for bringing fringe ideas, beliefs, and organizations into the mainstream. During his presidential campaign, Trump was accused of pandering to white supremacists. He retweeted open racists, and repeatedly refused to condemn David Duke, the Ku Klux Klan or white supremacists, in an interview on CNN's State of the Union, saying he would first need to "do research" because he knew nothing about Duke or white supremacists. Duke himself enthusiastically supported Trump throughout the 2016 primary and election, and has said he and like-minded people voted for Trump because of his promises to "take our country back".

After repeated questioning by reporters, Trump said he disavowed Duke and the Klan.

The alt-right movement coalesced around and enthusiastically supported Trump's candidacy, due in part to its opposition to multiculturalism and immigration.

In August 2016, he appointed Steve Bannon – the executive chairman of Breitbart News – as his campaign CEO; Bannon described Breitbart News as "the platform for the alt-right". In an interview days after the election, Trump condemned supporters who celebrated his victory with Nazi salutes.

Financial disclosures

As a candidate, Trump's FEC-required reports listed assets above $1.4 billion and outstanding debts of at least $315 million.

Trump has not released his tax returns, contrary to the practice of every major candidate since 1976 and his promises in 2014 and 2015 to do so if he ran for office. He said his tax returns were being audited (in actuality, audits do not prevent release of tax returns), and his lawyers had advised him against releasing them. Trump has told the press his tax rate is none of their business, and that he tries to pay "as little tax as possible".

In October 2016, portions of Trump's state filings for 1995 were leaked to a reporter from The New York Times. They show that Trump had declared a loss of $916 million that year, which could have let him avoid taxes for up to 18 years. During the second presidential debate, Trump acknowledged using the deduction, but declined to provide details such as the specific years it was applied.

On March 14, 2017, the first two pages of Trump's 2005 federal income tax returns were leaked to MSNBC. The document states that Trump had a gross adjusted income of $150 million and paid $38 million in federal taxes. The White House confirmed the authenticity of the documents.

In 2019, the House Ways and Means Committee sought Trump's personal and business tax returns from 2013 to 2018 from the Internal Revenue Service. Treasury Secretary Steven Mnuchin refused to turn over the documents, and ultimately defied a subpoena issued by the committee. A fall 2018 draft IRS legal memo asserted that tax returns must be provided to Congress upon request, unless a president invokes executive privilege, contradicting the administration's position.

Election to the presidency

On November 8, 2016, Trump received 306 pledged electoral votes versus 232 for Clinton. The official counts were 304 and 227 respectively, after defections on both sides. Trump received nearly 2.9 million fewer popular votes than Clinton, which made him the fifth person to be elected president while losing the popular vote. Clinton was ahead nationwide, with 65,853,514 votes (48.18%) compared to Trump's 62,984,828 votes (46.09%).

Trump's victory was a political upset. Polls had consistently shown Clinton with a nationwide – though diminishing – lead, as well as an advantage in most of the competitive states. Trump's support had been modestly underestimated, while Clinton's had been overestimated. The polls were relatively accurate, but media outlets and pundits alike showed overconfidence in a Clinton victory despite a large number of undecided voters and a favorable concentration of Trump's core constituencies in competitive states.

Trump won 30 states; included were Michigan, Pennsylvania, and Wisconsin, which had been part of what was considered a blue wall of Democratic strongholds since the 1990s. Clinton won 20 states and the District of Columbia. Trump's victory marked the return of an undivided Republican government – a Republican White House combined with Republican control of both chambers of Congress.

Trump is the oldest person to take office as president. He is also the first president who did not serve in the military or hold any government office prior to becoming president.

Protests

Some rallies during the primary season were accompanied by protests or violence, both inside and outside the venues. Trump's election victory sparked protests across the United States, in opposition to his policies and his inflammatory statements. Trump initially tweeted that these were "professional protesters, incited by the media" and "unfair", but later "Love the fact that the small groups of protesters last night have passion for our great country."

In the weeks following Trump's inauguration, massive anti-Trump demonstrations took place, such as the Women's Marches, which gathered 2.6 million people worldwide, including 500,000 in Washington alone. Marches against his travel ban began across the country on January 29, 2017, just nine days after his inauguration.

Presidency (2017–present)

Early actions

Trump was inaugurated as the 45th president of the United States on January 20, 2017. During his first week in office, he signed six executive orders: interim procedures in anticipation of repealing the Affordable Care Act ("Obamacare"), withdrawal from the Trans-Pacific Partnership negotiations, reinstatement of the Mexico City Policy, unlocking the Keystone XL and Dakota Access Pipeline construction projects, reinforcing border security, and beginning the planning and design process to construct a wall along the U.S. border with Mexico.

Upon inauguration, Trump delegated the management of his real estate business to his sons Eric and Donald Jr. His daughter Ivanka and her husband Jared Kushner became Assistant to the President and Senior Advisor to the President, respectively.

Energy and climate

Trump rejects the scientific consensus on climate change.He made large budget cuts to programs that research renewable energy and rolled back Obama-era policies directed at curbing climate change. In June 2017, Trump announced the withdrawal of the United States from the Paris Agreement, making the U.S. the only nation in the world to not ratify the agreement. At the 2019 G7 summit, Trump skipped the sessions on climate change but said afterward during a press conference that he is an environmentalist.

Trump has rolled back federal regulations aimed at curbing greenhouse gas emissions, air pollution, water pollution, and the usage of toxic substances. One example is the Clean Power Plan. He relaxed environmental standards for federal infrastructure projects, while expanding permitted areas for drilling and resource extraction, such as allowing drilling in the Arctic Refuge. Trump also weakened protections for animals. Trump's energy policies aimed to boost the production and exports of coal, oil, and natural gas.

Deregulation

During his presidency, Trump has dismantled many federal regulations on health, labor, and the environment, among other topics. Trump signed 15 Congressional Review Act resolutions repealing federal regulations, becoming the second president to sign a CRA resolution, and the first president to sign more than one CRA resolution. During his first six weeks in office, he delayed, suspended or reversed ninety federal regulations.

On January 30, 2017, Trump signed Executive Order 13771, which directed that for every new regulation administrative agencies issue "at least two prior regulations be identified for elimination". Agency defenders expressed opposition to Trump's criticisms, saying the bureaucracy exists to protect people against well-organized, well-funded interest groups.

Health care

During his campaign, Trump vowed to repeal and replace the Affordable Care Act, and shortly after taking office, Trump urged Congress to do so. In May 2017, the Republican-controlled House of

Representatives passed legislation to repeal the ACA in a party-line vote, but repeal proposals were narrowly voted down in the Senate after three Republicans joined all Democrats in opposing it.

Trump scaled back the implementation of the ACA through Executive Orders 13765 and 13813. Trump has expressed a desire to "let Obamacare fail"; his administration cut the ACA enrollment period in half and drastically reduced funding for advertising and other ways to encourage enrollment. The 2017 tax bill signed by Trump effectively repealed the ACA's individual health insurance mandate in 2019, and a budget bill Trump signed in 2019 repealed the Cadillac plan tax, medical device tax, and tanning tax. As president, Trump has falsely claimed he saved the coverage of pre-existing conditions provided by the ACA; in fact, the Trump administration has joined a lawsuit seeking to strike down the entire ACA, including protections for those with pre-existing conditions. If successful, the lawsuit would eliminate health insurance coverage for up to 23 million Americans. As a 2016 candidate, Trump promised to protect funding for Medicare and other social safety-net programs, but in January 2020 he suggested he was willing to consider cuts to such programs.

Social issues

Trump favored modifying the 2016 Republican platform opposing abortion, to allow for exceptions in cases of rape, incest, and circumstances endangering the health of the mother. He has said he is committed to appointing "pro-life" justices, pledging in 2016 to appoint justices who would "automatically" overturn Roe v. Wade. He says he personally supports "traditional marriage" but considers the nationwide legality of same-sex marriage a "settled" issue. Despite the statement by Trump and the White House saying they would keep in place a 2014 executive order from the Obama administration which created federal workplace protections for LGBT people, in March 2017, the Trump administration rolled back key components of the Obama administration's workplace protections for LGBT people.

Trump says he is opposed to gun control in general, although his views have shifted over time. After several mass shootings during his term, Trump initially said he would propose legislation to curtail gun violence, but abandoned the idea in November 2019. The Trump administration has taken an anti-marijuana position, revoking Obama-era policies that provided protections for states that legalized marijuana. Trump favors capital punishment; under Trump, the first federal execution in 17 years took place. Five more federal prisoners were executed, making the total number of federal executions under Trump higher than all of his predecessors combined going back to 1963. In 2016, Trump said he supported the use of waterboarding and "a hell of a lot worse" methods but later apparently recanted, at least partially, his support for torture due to the opposition of Defense Secretary James Mattis.

Pardons and commutations

In 2017, Trump pardoned former Arizona sheriff Joe Arpaio who was convicted of contempt of court for disobeying a court order to halt the racial profiling of Latinos. In 2018, Trump pardoned former Navy sailor Kristian Saucier, who was convicted of taking classified photographs of a submarine; Scooter Libby, a political aide to former vice president Dick Cheney, who was convicted of obstruction of justice, perjury, and making false statements to the FBI; conservative commentator Dinesh D'Souza, who had made illegal political campaign contributions; and he commuted the life sentence of Alice Marie Johnson, a non-violent drug trafficking offender, following a request by celebrity Kim Kardashian. In February 2020, Trump pardoned white-collar criminals Michael Milken, Bernard Kerik, and Edward J. DeBartolo Jr., and commuted former Illinois governor Rod Blagojevich's 14-year corruption sentence. July 2020, Trump commuted the 40-month sentence for his friend and adviser Roger Stone, who had been soon due to report to prison for covering up for Trump during the investigation into Russian interference in the 2016 presidential elections. In November 2020, Trump pardoned his former national security advisor Michael Flynn who had pleaded guilty of lying to the FBI.

Lafayette Square protester removal and photo op

On June 1, 2020, federal law enforcement officials used batons, rubber bullets, pepper spray projectiles, stun grenades, and smoke to remove a largely peaceful crowd of protesters from Lafayette Square, outside the White House. The removal had been ordered by Attorney General William Barr. Trump then walked to St. John's Episcopal Church. He posed for photographs holding a Bible, with Cabinet members and other officials later joining him in photos.

Religious leaders condemned the treatment of protesters and the photo opportunity itself. Many retired military leaders and defense officials condemned Trump's proposal to use the U.S. military against the protesters. The chairman of the Joint Chiefs of Staff, General Mark A. Miley, later apologized for accompanying Trump on the walk and thereby "creating the perception of the military involved in domestic politics".

Immigration

Trump's proposed immigration policies were a topic of bitter and contentious debate during the campaign. He promised to build a more substantial wall on the Mexico–United States border to keep out illegal immigrants and vowed Mexico would pay for it. He pledged to massively deport illegal immigrants residing in the United States, and criticized birthright citizenship for creating "anchor babies". As president, he frequently described illegal immigration as an "invasion" and conflated immigrants with the gang MS-13, though research shows undocumented immigrants have a lower crime rate than native-born Americans.

Travel ban

Following the 2015 San Bernardino attack, Trump made a controversial proposal to ban Muslim foreigners from entering the United States until stronger vetting systems could be implemented. He later reframed the proposed ban to apply to countries with a "proven history of terrorism".

On January 27, 2017, Trump signed Executive Order 13769, which suspended admission of refugees for 120 days and denied entry to citizens of Iraq, Iran, Libya, Somalia, Sudan, Syria, and Yemen for 90 days, citing security concerns. The order took effect immediately and without warning. Confusion and protests caused chaos at airports. Sally Yates, the acting Attorney General, directed Justice Department lawyers not to defend the executive order, which she deemed unenforceable and unconstitutional; Trump immediately dismissed her. Multiple legal challenges were filed against the order, and a federal judge blocked its implementation nationwide. On March 6, Trump issued a revised order, which excluded Iraq, gave specific exemptions for permanent residents, and removed priorities for Christian minorities. Again federal judges in three states blocked its implementation. In a decision in June 2017, the

Supreme Court ruled that the ban could be enforced on visitors who lack a "credible claim of a bona fide relationship with a person or entity in the United States".

The temporary order was replaced by Presidential Proclamation 9645 on September 24, 2017, which permanently restricts travel from the originally targeted countries except Iraq and Sudan, and further bans travelers from North Korea and Chad, along with certain Venezuelan officials. After lower courts partially blocked the new restrictions, the Supreme Court allowed the September version to go into full effect on December 4, 2017, and ultimately upheld the travel ban in a June 2019 ruling.

Family separation at border

The Trump administration has separated more than 5,400 migrant children from their parents at the U.S.–Mexico border while the families attempted to enter the U.S. The Trump administration sharply increased the number of family separations at the border starting from the summer of 2017, before an official policy was announced in 2018; this was not reported publicly until January 2019.

In April 2018, the Trump administration announced a "zero tolerance" policy whereby every adult suspected of illegal entry would be criminally prosecuted. This resulted in family separations, as the migrant adults were put in criminal detention for prosecution, while their children were taken away as unaccompanied alien minors. The children would be brought to immigration detention, immigrant shelters, tent camps, or metal cages, with the stated aim of releasing them to relatives or sponsors. Administration officials described the policy as a way to deter illegal immigration.

The policy of family separations had no precedent in previous administrations and sparked public outrage, with Democrats, Republicans, Trump allies, and religious groups demanding that the policy be rescinded. Trump falsely asserted that his administration was merely following the law, blaming Democrats, when in fact this was his administration's policy. More than 2,300 children were separated as a result of the "zero tolerance policy", the Trump administration revealed in June 2018.

Although Trump originally argued that the issue could not be solved via executive order, he proceeded to sign an executive order on June 20, 2018, mandating that migrant families be detained together, unless the administration judged that doing so would harm the child. On June 26, 2018, a federal judge concluded that the Trump administration had "no system in place to keep track of" the separated children, nor any effective measures for family communication and reunification; the judge ordered for the families to be reunited, and family separations stopped, except in the cases where the parent(s) are judged unfit to take care of the child, or if there is parental approval.

In 2019, the Trump administration reported that 4,370 children were separated from July 2017 to June 2018. Even after the June 2018 federal court order, the Trump administration continued to practice family separations, with more than a thousand migrant children separated.

Migrant detentions

While the Obama administration detained and deported migrants at high rates, the Trump administration took it to a significantly higher level.

The Department of Homeland Security Office of Inspector General inspections of migrant detention centers in 2018 and 2019 found that U.S. Customs and Border Protection (CBP) "in many instances" violated federal guidelines for detaining migrant children for too long before passing them to the Office of Refugee Resettlement and that migrants were detained for prolonged periods under dangerous conditions failing federal standards, enduring dangerous overcrowding and poor hygiene and food. CBP Commissioner Kevin MacLennan said in 2019 that there was a "border security and a humanitarian crisis" and that the immigration system was at a "breaking point".

The treatment of the detained migrants resulted in a public outcry by July 2019. That month, Trump reacted to criticism of the migrant detentions by saying if the migrants were unhappy about the conditions of the detention facilities, "just tell them not to come."

In August 2019, the administration attempted to change the 1997 Flores Agreement that limits detention of migrant families to 20 days; the new policy allowing indefinite detention was blocked before it would go into effect.

2018–2019 federal government shutdown

On December 22, 2018, the federal government was partially shut down after Trump declared that any funding extension must include $5.6 billion in federal funds for a U.S.–Mexico border wall to partly fulfill his campaign promise. The shutdown was caused by a lapse in funding for nine federal departments, affecting about one-fourth of federal government activities. Trump said he would not accept any bill that did not include funding for the wall, and Democrats, who control the House, said they would not support any bill that does. Senate Republicans have said they will not advance any legislation Trump would not sign. In earlier negotiations with Democratic leaders, Trump commented that he would be "proud to shut down the government for border security".

As a result of the shutdown, about 380,000 government employees were furloughed and 420,000 government employees worked without pay. According to a CBO estimate, the shutdown resulted in a permanent loss of $3 billion to the U.S. economy. About half of Americans blamed Trump for the shutdown, and Trump's approval ratings dropped.

On January 25, 2019, Congress unanimously approved a temporary funding bill that provided no funds for the wall but would provide delayed paychecks to government workers. Trump signed the bill that day, ending the shutdown at 35 days. It was the longest U.S. government shutdown in history.

Since the government funding was temporary, another shutdown loomed. On February 14, 2019, Congress approved a funding bill that included $1.375 billion for 55 miles of border fences, in lieu of Trump's intended wall. Trump signed the bill the next day.

National emergency regarding the southern border

On February 15, 2019, after Trump received from Congress only $1.375 billion for border fencing after demanding $5.7 billion for the Trump wall, he declared a National Emergency Concerning the Southern Border of the United States, in hopes of getting another $6.7 billion without congressional approval, using funds for military construction, drug interdiction, and money from the Treasury. In doing so, Trump acknowledged that he "didn't need to" declare a national emergency, but he "would rather do it much faster".

Congress twice passed resolutions to block Trump's national emergency declarations, but Trump vetoed both and there were not enough votes in Congress for a veto override. Trump's decision to divert other government funding to fund the wall resulted in legal challenges. In July 2019, the Supreme Court allowed Trump to use $2.5 billion (originally meant for anti-drug programs) from the Department of Defense to build the Trump wall. In December 2019, a federal judge stopped the Trump administration from using $3.6 billion of military construction funds for the Trump wall.

Trump wall

As a presidential candidate, Trump promised to construct a wall along the U.S.–Mexico border to prevent migration. In 2017, the border had 654 miles of primary fencing, 37 miles of secondary fencing and 14 miles of tertiary fencing. Trump's target, from 2015 to 2017, was 1,000 miles of wall. The Trump administration set a target of 450 miles of new or renovated barriers by December 2020, with an ultimate goal of 509 miles of new or renovated barriers by August 2021. Even into 2020, Trump has repeatedly provided false assertions that Mexico is paying for the Trump wall, although American taxpayers are footing the bill from funds being diverted from the U.S. Department of Defense.

In October 2018, the administration revealed two miles of replacement fences made of steel posts, which it called the first section of Trump's 'wall', although earlier that year Border Patrol had said the project was unrelated to the Trump wall and had been long planned (dating to 2009). In December 2018 and January 2019, Trump tweeted out a design of a steel fence, and a picture of a fence, while declaring "the wall is coming."

By November 2019, the Trump administration had replaced around 78 miles of the Mexico–United States barrier along the border; these replacement barriers were not walls, but fences made of bollards. The administration in November 2019 said it had "just started breaking ground" to build new barriers in areas where no structure existed. By May 2020, the Trump administration had replaced 172 miles of dilapidated or outdated design barriers, and constructed 15 miles of new border barriers.

Foreign policy

Trump describes himself as a "nationalist" and his foreign policy as "America First". He has espoused isolationist, non-interventionist, and protectionist views.

His foreign policy has been marked by repeated praise and support of neo-nationalist and authoritarian strongmen and criticism of democratic governments. Trump has cited Israel's Benjamin Netanyahu, the Philippines' Rodrigo Duterte, Egypt's Abdel Fattah el-Sisi, Turkey's Tayyip Erdoğan, Russia's Vladimir

Putin, King Salman of Saudi Arabia, Brazil's Jair Bolsonaro, Italy's Giuseppe Conte, India's Narendra Modi, Hungary's Viktor Orbán, and Poland's Andrzej Duda as examples of good leaders.

As a candidate, Trump questioned the need for NATO as president, he repeatedly and publicly criticized NATO and the U.S.'s NATO allies, and has privately suggested on multiple occasions that the United States should withdraw from NATO. Hallmarks of foreign relations during Trump's tenure include unpredictability and uncertainty, a lack of a consistent foreign policy, and strained and sometimes antagonistic relationships with the U.S.'s European allies.

Impeachment

Impeachment by the House of Representatives

During much of Trump's presidency, Democrats were divided on the question of impeachment. Fewer than 20 representatives in the House supported impeachment by January 2019; after the Mueller Report was released in April and special counsel Robert Mueller testified in July, this number grew to around 140 representatives.

In August 2019, a whistleblower filed a complaint with the Inspector General of the Intelligence Community about a July 25 phone call between Trump and President of Ukraine Volodymyr Zelensky, during which Trump had pressured Zelensky to investigate CrowdStrike and Democratic presidential primary candidate Joe Biden and his son Hunter, adding that the White House had attempted to cover-up the incident. The whistleblower further stated that the call was part of a wider pressure campaign by Trump's personal attorney Giuliani and the Trump administration which may have included withholding financial aid from Ukraine in July 2019 and canceling Vice President Pence's May 2019 Ukraine trip. Trump later confirmed having withheld military aid from Ukraine and offered contradictory reasons for the decision.

House speaker Nancy Pelosi initiated a formal impeachment inquiry on September 24, 2019. The Trump administration subsequently released a memorandum of the July 25 phone call, confirming that after Zelensky mentioned purchasing American anti-tank missiles, Trump asked Zelensky to investigate and to discuss these matters with Giuliani and Attorney General Barr. The testimony of multiple administration officials and former officials confirmed that this was part of a broader effort to further Trump's personal interests by giving him an advantage in the upcoming presidential election. In October 2019, William B. Taylor Jr., the chargé d'affaires for Ukraine, testified before congressional committees that soon after arriving in Ukraine in June 2019, he found that Zelensky was being subjected to pressure directed by Trump and led by Giuliani. According to Taylor and others, the goal was to coerce Zelensky into making a public commitment to investigate the company that employed Hunter Biden, as well as rumors about Ukrainian involvement in the 2016 U.S. presidential election. He said it was made clear that until Zelensky made such an announcement, the administration would not release scheduled military aid for Ukraine and not invite Zelensky to the White House. Zelensky denied that he felt pressured by Trump.

In December 2019, the House Intelligence Committee published a report authored by Democrats on the committee, stating that "the impeachment inquiry has found that President Trump, personally and acting through agents ... solicited the interference of a foreign government, Ukraine, to benefit his reelection." The report said Trump had withheld military aid and a White House invitation to pressure Ukraine to announce investigations into Trump's political rivals. Furthermore, the report stated that Trump "openly and indiscriminately" defied impeachment proceedings by telling his administration officials to ignore subpoenas. 8,208 House Republicans released a draft of a countering report the previous day, saying that the evidence "does not prove any of these Democrat allegations."

On December 13, 2019, the House Judiciary Committee voted along party lines to pass two articles of impeachment: abuse of power and obstruction of

Congress. After debate, the House of Representatives impeached Trump with both articles on December 18.

Impeachment trial in the Senate

The Senate impeachment trial began on January 16, 2020. On January 22, the Republican Senate majority rejected amendments proposed by the Democratic minority to call witnesses and subpoena documents; evidence collected during the House impeachment proceedings was entered into the Senate record.

For three days, January 22–24, the impeachment managers for the House presented their case to the Senate. They cited evidence to support charges of abuse of power and obstruction of Congress, and asserted that Trump's actions were exactly what the founding fathers had in mind when they created the Constitution's impeachment process.

Responding over the next three days, the Trump legal team did not deny the facts as presented in the charges but said Trump had not broken any laws or obstructed Congress. They argued that the impeachment was "constitutionally and legally invalid" because Trump was not charged with a crime and that abuse of power is not an impeachable offense.

On January 31, the Senate voted against allowing subpoenas for witnesses or documents; 51 Republicans formed the majority for this vote. Thus, this became the first impeachment trial in U.S. history without witness testimony. On February 5, Trump was acquitted of both charges in a vote nearly along party lines, with Republican Mitt Romney voting to convict on one of the charges, "abuse of power".

Following his acquittal, Trump began removing impeachment witnesses and political appointees and career officials he deemed insufficiently loyal.

2020 presidential election

Breaking with precedent, Trump filed to run for a second term as president by filing with the FEC within a few hours of assuming the presidency. Trump held his first re-election rally less than a month after taking office. In his first two years in office, Trump's reelection committee reported raising $67.5 million, allowing him to begin 2019 with $19.3 million cash on hand. From the beginning of 2019 through July 2020, the Trump campaign and Republican Party raised $1.1 billion, but spent $800 million of that amount, evaporating their formerly large cash advantage over the Democratic nominee, former vice president Joe Biden. The campaign's cash crunch forced a scale-back in advertising spending.

Starting in spring 2020, Trump began to sow doubts about the election, repeatedly claiming without evidence that the election would be "rigged" and expected widespread use of mail balloting would produce "massive election fraud". In what The New York Times called an "extraordinary breach of presidential decorum", on July 30 Trump raised the idea of delaying the election. When in August the

House of Representatives voted for a $25 billion grant to the U.S. Postal Service for the expected surge in mail voting, Trump blocked funding, saying he wanted to prevent any increase in voting by mail. Trump became the Republican nominee on August 24, 2020. He repeatedly refused to say whether he would accept the results of the election and commit to a peaceful transition of power if he lost.

Trump campaign advertisements focused on crime, claiming that cities would descend into lawlessness if his opponent, Biden, won the presidency. Trump repeatedly misrepresented Biden's positions during the campaign. Trump's campaign message shifted to racist rhetoric in an attempt to reclaim voters lost from his base.

The results of the election held on November 3 were unclear for several days. On November 7, major news organizations projected Biden as the winner. On December 5, Biden led Trump in the national vote count 81.3 million (51.3%) to 74.2 million (46.9%). Biden is projected to win the Electoral College 306 to 232. U.S. election officials said the election was the "most secure" in U.S. history.

At 2 a.m. the morning after the election, with the results still unclear, Trump declared victory. After Biden was projected the winner days later, Trump said, "this election is far from over" and alleged election fraud without providing evidence. By the end of November he had filed over 50 legal challenges in key states, but most of them had been dismissed by the courts. His legal team led by Rudy Giuliani made numerous false and unsubstantiated assertions about an international communist conspiracy, rigged voting machines and polling place fraud to claim the election had been stolen from Trump. Trump blocked government officials from cooperating in the presidential transition of Joe Biden.

The misinformation spread by Trump and his allies and their unsubstantiated legal claims were aimed at causing chaos and confusion and also, according to some Trump allies, ensuring the continued loyalty of Trump supporters. Trump's allegations of widespread voting fraud were refuted by judges, state election officials, and his own administration's Cybersecurity and Infrastructure Security Agency (CISA). After CISA director Chris Krebs contradicted Trump's voting fraud allegations, Trump fired him on November 17.

With his post-election legal challenges to the election of Biden failing, Trump withdrew from public activities and drew criticism that, given the surge in the pandemic, his retreat was being perceived as irresponsible sulking. On November 23, 2020, the administrator of the General Services Administration declared Biden to be the apparent winner of the election, allowing the disbursement of transition resources to his team. Trump, while not formally conceding, announced his approval of the decision on Twitter and later confirmed that he would leave the White House. However, Trump also personally contacted Republican legislators or governors in the states of Michigan, Georgia, and Pennsylvania, in an attempt to overturn his election losses in those states, one strategy being to try to get the states' presidential electors replaced.

Donald Trump Inspirational Quotes

"Sometimes your best investments are the ones you don't make."

- **Donald Trump**

"What separates the winners from the losers is how a person reacts to each new twist of fate."

- **Donald Trump**

"It's a blip, not a catastrophe."

- **Donald Trump**

"As long as you are going to be thinking anyway, think big."

- **Donald Trump**

"I don't hire a lot of number-crunchers, and I don't trust fancy marketing surveys. I do my own surveys and draw my own conclusions."

- **Donald Trump**

"Everything in life is luck."

- **Donald Trump**

"If you are a little different, or a little outrageous, or if you do things that are bold or controversial, the press is going to write about you."

- **Donald Trump**

"A tiny leak can sink a ship."

- **Donald Trump**

"When you are wronged repeatedly, the worst thing you can do is continue taking it--fight back!"

- **Donald Trump**

"Courage is not the absence of fear. Courage is the ability to act effectively, in spite of fear."

- **Donald Trump**

"Remember, there's no such thing as an unrealistic goal--just unrealistic time frames."

- **Donald Trump**

"Criticism is easier to take when you realize that the only people who aren't criticized are those who don't take risks."

- **Donald Trump**

"I only work with the best."

- **Donald Trump**

"Leaders, true leaders, take responsibility for the success of the team, and understand that they must also take responsibility for the failure."

- **Donald Trump**

"Money was never a big motivation for me, except as a way to keep score. The real excitement is playing the game."

- **Donald Trump**

"Sometimes by losing a battle you find a new way to win the war."

- **Donald Trump**

"Nothing great in the world has been accomplished without passion."

- **Donald Trump**

"Rules are meant to be broken."

- **Donald Trump**

"Your business, and your brand, must first let people know what you care about, and that you care about them."

- **Donald Trump**

"In the end, you're measured not by how much you undertake, but by what you finally accomplish."

- **Donald Trump**

"Anyone who thinks my story is anywhere near over is sadly mistaken."

- **Donald Trump**

Printed in Great Britain
by Amazon